Henry VII'

JAMES WILKINSON

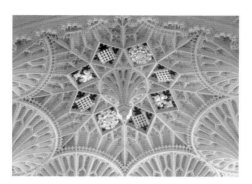

FRONT COVER: The fan vaulting, designed by William Vertue, is the crowning glory of Henry VII's Chapel.

OPPOSITE: A frieze of angels and Tudor emblems decorates the Chapel, which was consecrated in 1516.

A Chapel 'worthy of the Virgin Mary'

KING HENRY VII's LADY CHAPEL is the crowning glory of Westminster Abbey. With its spectacular vault and hanging pendants, it is unique and stands in complete contrast to the rest of the Abbey's plainer and earlier Gothic architecture. Its intricate decoration, colourful banners, superb early Tudor stalls, Renaissance tombs and royal sepulchres make it one of the most historic chapels in Britain. Built between 1503 and about 1512, it represented a departure in style. In 1545 John Leland called it 'the wonder of the entire world' (*miraculum orbis universali*). And though not every-one approved (the diarist John Evelyn referred to it dismissively as 'crinkle crankle') most did, and today's visitors stand in awe as they must have done 500 years ago when it was completed. Indeed it was once even more glorious than it is now, laden as it was with precious furnishings and tapestries, most of which disappeared in 1540 and in 1548 at the dissolution of the Abbey and the abolition of chantries. But even without these embellishments its impact is immediate and impressive.

A finial decorating
Queen Elizabeth I's tomb.

OPPOSITE: The exquisite fan
vaulting with its hanging pendants
helped make the Chapel
'the wonder of the entire world'.

The Chapel as we know it today was not the first Lady Chapel in the Abbey. In the 13th century the monks had a particular devotion to St Mary the Virgin and venerated her at a special altar where the daily Lady Mass was sung by the monks. A second altar dedicated to her was probably situated in a chapel just north of the north transept, which was the ceremonial entrance to the church. The chapel enabled people to hear Mass without having to enter the church. But the monks decided they wanted something more worthy of the Virgin Mary and so began work on a fine new Lady Chapel to the east of Edward the Confessor's Romanesque Abbey. The foundation stone was laid on 16 May 1220 by the 13-year-old King Henry III. The chapel was about the same size as the present one without the side aisles. Having built it at their own expense, the monks had to sustain it, and so acquired property nearby which produced rents of about £20 a year, most of which went on wax for candles.

Some 25 years later when his Lady Chapel was nearing completion, Henry III decided to pull down Edward the Confessor's Abbey and replace it with the most glorious church in the Gothic style in England. In order

3

to incorporate the Lady Chapel into the new structure, in 1256 its height was raised at its west end. This Chapel, with its ever more elaborate worship, lasted for 250 years until, at the beginning of the 16th century, Henry VII decided to replace it.

Henry had defeated Richard III at the Battle of Bosworth Field in 1485, but his claim to the throne was tenuous. An arranged marriage with Elizabeth of York had helped consolidate his position but more was needed. At about this time a cult was developing around the murdered King Henry VI (died 1471) who was Henry VII's father's half-brother. Though buried initially at Chertsey Abbey, his body had been moved to Windsor in 1483. Henry VII decided to exploit this cult by seeking saint-hood for the dead King and then reburying him in a special new Lady Chapel he was building in the 1490s at the east end of St George's Chapel, Windsor, which he had intended would also be his own resting place. The monks at both Chertsey and Westminster protested – the Westminster monks claimed that Henry VI had wanted to be buried at Westminster and they stressed the long tradition of royal burials at the Abbey. A judicial inquiry followed which, in 1498, found in favour of Westminster, so Henry began developing a similar shrine at the Abbey for his uncle's remains, where Masses would be said and alms given. The Abbey even paid £500 to ensure that the papal licence for the transfer of the body was granted, and to cover the expenses of the removal. The new Chapel at Westminster was started in January 1503. In his will Henry VII had made clear his reasons for building the Chapel: to honour the Virgin, as a tomb for himself and his queen and descendants, and as an honourable resting place for his uncle. He ordered that the Chapel should be richly painted and that no expense was to be spared. He and his mother, Lady Margaret Beaufort, lavished money on it to a total of more than £14,000. Henry planned that Henry VI would lie in a shrine behind the main altar, while his own remains and those of his wife would lie in a specially made bronze chantry chapel in front of the altar. But there was a hold-up: the infamous Pope Julius II (1503–13) was asking too much money for the canonisation.

After Henry VII died in 1509, his son, Henry VIII, had no interest in canonising Henry VI whose body remained at Windsor. Meanwhile Henry VII's magnificent tomb by the Italian, Pietro Torrigiano, was installed in its chantry behind the main altar – the position originally earmarked for Henry VI's shrine. Henry VIII later commissioned Torrigiano to design an even more splendid tomb for himself at Westminster, but it was never completed and Henry VIII was buried at Windsor.

Henry VII's head from his funeral effigy is based on a death mask.

OPPOSITE: Wooden statue of Henry VI on the north-west return stall.

Building the Chapel

WHEN THE FIRST LADY CHAPEL was demolished between October 1502 and January 1503 the monks had to decide what to do with some of the remains which had been buried there. Prominent among these was the body of Katherine de Valois, the wife of Henry V. Her coffin was removed and placed near the tomb of her husband, east of Edward the Confessor's shrine. It is probable that Henry VII had intended to re-bury her in his new Chapel, but it was never done and her coffin remained on display for over 200 years. One who saw her body in 1585 described it as being like an Egyptian mummy, and Samuel Pepys, writing in his diary in 1669, said he kissed her on the lips, adding '… this was my birthday, thirty-six years old that I did first kiss a Queen'. The coffin was later hidden away and in 1878 was finally buried beneath the altar table in Henry V's chantry chapel.

One of many brass heraldic pennants on the Chapel's roof.

OPPOSITE: Instead of conventional stone walls the Chapel has undulating glazed screens – derided as 'crinkle crankle' by the diarist John Evelyn.

Another coffin, displaced when the old Chapel was demolished, was that of Anne Mowbray (1472–1481), who had married one of the 'Princes in the Tower', Richard, Duke of York, when they were both only five years old. It had always been assumed she had been re-buried in the new Chapel but in 1964 her coffin was found in a vault on the site of a medieval nunnery many miles away in Stepney in East London. She was re-interred in Henry VII's Chapel in 1965.

With the old Lady Chapel demolished, the foundation stone of Henry VII's new Lady Chapel was laid at 2.45pm on 24 January 1503 by Abbot John Islip. Though we know exactly when it was laid and who was present at the ceremony, no-one knows where the stone is now.

The Chapel was probably designed in two parts. The lower part is thought to have been the work of Robert Janyns, who had previously designed and built a fine tower at Windsor Castle; or it may have been Robert Vertue who, as a mason, had earlier worked on the Abbey's nave. The architecture was radical for the time. Instead of conventional stone walls the architect opted for undulating glazed screens. Both Robert Janyns and Robert Vertue died in 1506, possibly from the plague, and it is thought that Robert Vertue's brother, William, continued the work. It is probably him we have to thank for the spectacular vault with its pendants.

In the 1990s much of the decaying exterior stonework of the Chapel was replaced with hundreds of newly carved beasts, crockets and other architectural features.

The Chapel was finally consecrated in 1516 and for a very short time elaborate Masses were sung here.

The Chapel was embellished with badges and heraldic devices reflecting its provenance, including the Beaufort portcullis, the English lion, French fleur-de-lis, the Welsh dragon and the Tudor rose. These badges and images appear on the massive doors made of bronze mounted on wood, the grille of the chantry and on some of the stonework. They also originally decorated the stained glass windows, designed by the craftsman Barnard Flower, which were were among the finest in England. Traces of the glass images were still in evidence until they were finally destroyed in the Second World War. Barnard Flower designed similar windows to those in Henry VII's Chapel for the Chapel of King's College, Cambridge, and these have survived. In addition to the heraldic devices, the Lady Chapel's original windows probably also included Gospel scenes and Old Testament subjects. Today there are two main stained glass windows in the Chapel. The great west window was unveiled by the

Queen in 1995 to mark the completion of the 22-year restoration of the Abbey. It contains the initials, cyphers and coats of arms of those involved in the Westminster Abbey Trust, which raised money for the restoration programme, and of some of the donors. The arms of the Sovereign appear in the centre, flanked on the south by those of the Duke of Edinburgh, who chaired the Trust and on the north by those of Prince Charles, the Great Master of the order of knighthood known as the Most Honourable Order of the Bath, whose Chapel this has been since 1725.

The central east window which celebrates the Blessed Virgin Mary was designed by Alan Younger and was dedicated on 22 November 2000. It includes a nativity scene in the lower panels. The Star of Bethlehem is depicted as the Hale Bopp comet which was passing over the home of the designer as he worked on the window. In the bottom right-hand corner are the kneeling figures of the donors of this window, Lord and Lady Harris of Peckham.

The aisles also contain small modern stained glass windows marking the generosity of individuals who contributed towards the cost of the Abbey's restoration.

Though the Chapel was originally sumptuously furnished, none of the proposed painting of the Chapel's interior was carried out. Henry VII died in 1509, leaving the Chapel unfinished and, even though he had asked in his will for the decoration to be done, his son and successor, Henry VIII, ignored it. It was only in the late twentieth century that some gilding was added to the pendant bosses by the restoring architect, Donald Buttress.

The Chapel's massive bronze-covered wooden doors are embellished with badges and heraldic symbols, including the Tudor rose and the Beaufort portcullis.

The small chapel north of the chantry was probably designed as an oratory for Henry VII.

OPPOSITE: The Chapel, after Canaletto, showing the original stone screens beyond the wooden stalls.

At the east end of the Lady Chapel are five small radiating chapels, each of which originally had an altar. Today only the eastern-most chapel has one.

The two chapels adjacent to the wooden stalls have small doors in them. These doors are set not in the centre of the screening wall but at one end, which implies that each chapel was designed as an oratory where members of the royal family could go to pray in private, close to what was intended to be the altar to 'St' Henry VI. The one on the north side was probably designed for Henry VII himself to pray in. Originally these two chapels and those next to them had bowed stone screens, with windows in them, which extended upwards, but they were cut down to the present size in 1806. These stone screens can be seen in an eighteenth-century print based on a picture of the Chapel by Canaletto.

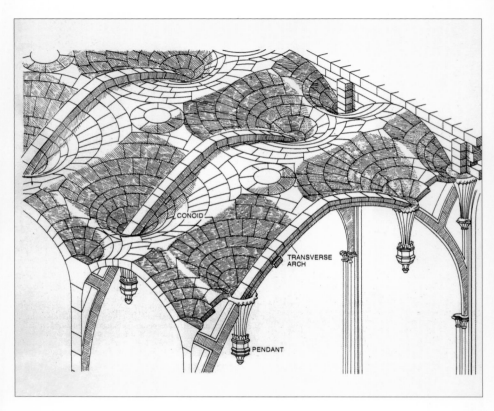

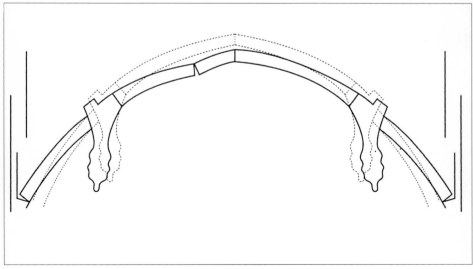

The most striking feature in the Chapel is the great vault but architecturally, all is not what it seems. Careful measurement has revealed that the pendants are not hanging exactly vertically, as one would expect. In the decades after the building was complete there was slight movement as the building settled owing to pressure from the masonry in the vault and slight movement of the foundations of the buttresses as the soil compacted. This caused the vault span to increase slightly, allowing some of the interlinking stones in the vault to drop a little. The result is that the pendants are slightly splayed. These defects probably occurred by 1550, since when there has been little shift in the stonework. The fact that the Chapel's vault mostly survived the shock of bombs exploding close by during the Second World War with relatively little damage (only two pendants crashed to the floor) shows the basic strength of the construction.

The hanging pendants in the fan vaulting were gilded during the most recent restoration of the Chapel.

OPPOSITE TOP: Isometric drawing showing how the vault was constructed.

OPPOSITE BELOW: The pendants splayed in the sixteenth century due to settlement.

The King's tomb and chantry chapel

THE CHANTRY CHAPEL, WHICH CONTAINS the tomb of Henry VII and Elizabeth of York, was in effect a chapel within a chapel. Designed by Thomas Ducheman (Thomas the Dutchman), it was begun about 1505, four years before Henry VII's death, and was made in pieces, each with a series of slashes and zeros which enabled it to be reconstructed around the tomb. Inside the chantry, there is a lengthy inscription around the frieze and a similar one on the outside. Also on the outside were 32 bronze statues, four each on the east and west walls, and 12 each on the north and south sides. Only six now survive. They include St James the Greater with pilgrim's hat and scallop shell, St Edward the Confessor, St Bartholomew carrying his flayed skin over his arm, St John the Evangelist holding a chalice and St George in armour with a dragon biting his leg.

At the east end of the chantry chapel is a small step, or pace, on which once stood the chapel's altar. Above it and extending across from one side of the chantry to the other is a bar – all that is left of the structure which once supported the canopy over the altar.

Bronze figures on the grille include, from left, St James the Greater with his pilgrim's hat, St George in armour, and St John the evangelist with a chalice.

OPPOSITE: Torrigiano's effigy of Henry VII on his magnificent Renaissance tomb.

In his will Henry VII was very specific about how he wanted the altar furnished. It was clearly to be a glorious sight. Above the altar there was to be a reredos slightly wider than the altar on which there should be a rood (*ie* a crucifix) and statues of Mary and John with as many images of saints as would fit and, beneath, statues of the 12 apostles carved in wood and covered with plates of gold. Henry also gave to the altar a piece of the Holy Cross, encased in gold and garnished with pearls and precious stones, and a second relic, one of the legs of St George, set in silver gilt. He wanted these placed on the altar on special feast days. In addition he made provision for the altar to have an elaborately illuminated hand-written Mass book, three altar cloths, vestments, a golden chalice, cruets, candlesticks, pictures, basins and bells. The other altars in the Lady Chapel were to be similarly equipped.

The chantry altar was used exclusively for masses at 7.00am and 8.00am and immediately after the singing of the Gospel at the High Mass in the main Chapel.

RIGHT: Gilt bronze cherubs support the royal arms at the east end of the tomb.

The complete grille forming the chantry chapel enclosing the tomb of Henry VII and Elizabeth of York.

16

Inside the chantry are Torrigiano's superb effigies of Henry VII and his wife on a large tomb chest. It is a remarkable Renaissance structure in complete contrast to the tombs of previous kings and queens buried in the Abbey. It is made of Tournai marble and has, on the north and south sides, carefully carved wreaths around bronze medallions featuring pairs of saints and other religious figures. There are gilt bronze angels on the corners and at the east end is a pair of putti holding ribbons from which is suspended the royal coat of arms. The effigies of the King and Queen, in accordance with Henry's instructions, are made of gilt bronze, and had to be 'as good or better than any of the other kings and queens in the Abbey.' In fact, the bodies of the King and Queen lie not within the tomb but in a specially built vault beneath it.

Position of the lead coffins in the burial vault beneath the tomb, from left: James I, Elizabeth of York, and Henry VII.

OPPOSITE: The gilt bronze effigies of the King and Queen, with gilt cherubs at each corner of the tomb.

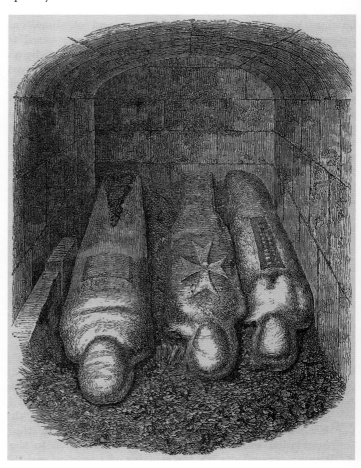

18

Henry's wife, Elizabeth, predeceased him in 1503 and was first buried in a temporary vault in the crossing of the Abbey in front of the high altar. After the King's death he was said to have been laid beside her but whether he too went into the crossing vault before being transferred into the Lady Chapel, or whether, after his death, they were both put in the vault where they now lie is not certain. The Henry VII vault was opened by Dean Stanley in 1869 during his search for the coffin of James I (died 1625). Henry VII's coffin was identified by its inscription, while his wife's coffin, which had no inscription, was identified by its Maltese cross. Originally these two coffins had lain either side of the mid-line of the vault. But in order to make room for James I's coffin they had been moved to the south side.

Henry VIII was buried at Windsor and it was the burial of his son, Edward VI, in the Lady Chapel that ensured that the Chapel became a royal mausoleum for the next 200 years. Edward was buried directly beneath the main altar. One reason, it has been suggested, is that the Catholic Mary I did not want any memorial erected over her Protestant half-brother and by putting him beneath the altar she pre-empted such a possibility. In fact a drawing of a monument attributed to Cornelius Cure and dated to the 1570s exists but it was never built. A modern plaque marks the King's burial place.

Elizabeth of York died in 1503, the year that the Chapel's foundation stone was laid.

OPPOSITE: Edward VI was buried beneath the altar. A monument to him was never built.

Pietro Torrigiano (1472–1528) was a Florentine sculptor with a fiery temper. It is said that, in 1492, he and Michelangelo were copying the frescoes in the Carmine Chapel when Torrigiano took offence at something that Michelangelo said and broke his nose in a fight. Torrigiano was banished from Florence. By 1507 he was in London.

In 1511 he signed a contract to design the tomb for Henry VII, mother Lady Margaret Beaufort (died 1509). Other commissions followed. In 1512 Henry VII commissioned him to build his tomb and paid him £1,500. In 1517 Torrigiano was asked to design the main altar for the Lady Chapel, for which he was paid £1,000.

Torrigiano came to a sad end. In 1525, while the sculptor was in Spain, he was swindled out of a large sum of money and was so angry that he destroyed a statue of the Virgin and Child which he had been carving. He was promptly arrested for sacrilege and imprisoned. Here he fell into a serious depression and starved to death.

King Henry VII instructs the monks

A Tudor rose on the cover of the indentures, which set out how the King was to be honoured by the monks.

BUILDING THE CHAPEL WAS ONLY THE FIRST PART of Henry VII's plans for the future. He made sure that after his death his soul and that of his wife would benefit from a whole series of commitments entered into by the monks. They took the form of binding contracts between the King and monks which set out in great detail exactly how the King and Queen were to be honoured. His elaborate will also gave many details of what he wanted.

The indentures, which date from 1504, stipulated, for example, that the monks had to pray for the king's safety and well-being during his lifetime and for the salvation of his soul after death. Three extra monks were to be employed to devote themselves entirely to the special services to be held in the chantry chapel.

Great stress was laid on the burning of candles around the tomb. Throughout the year four candles, initially eleven feet high, had to burn continuously and be replaced when they had burned down to six feet. They were set in the four large brackets which still branch out in the middle of each side of the chantry grille, though some extra brackets must have been necessary to support them. At certain services, such as High Mass and at Evensong on major feast days, 30 candles, each taller than a man, were to burn around the top of the chantry and be replaced when they had burned down to five feet (the lower limit was set possibly because it had been noticed that on the anniversaries of the deaths of previous kings and queens the monks had become rather lax and had let the candles burn down too far). For the annual anniversary services, like those held to commemorate Henry III, Eleanor of Castille, Richard II, Anne of Bohemia and Henry V, no expense was to be spared. No fewer than 100 candles, each weighing 12 lbs and nine feet tall, were to be lit.

To make sure that the monks fulfilled their side of the contract the indentures set out the fines they faced if they neglected their duties. For example, if one of the four large candles remained unlit for half an hour during the day the monks would be fined 3s 4d. If the monks failed to deliver a weekly sermon they were to be fined five marks. Failure to ring

One of the large brackets on the grille surrounding Henry VII's tomb where candles were burned continuously.

BELOW: Monks at the sixteenth-century funeral of Abbot John Islip as depicted in the Islip Roll.

the bell for the chantry Mass would incur a fine of one mark. The contract was to be supervised and fines administered by the other parties to the agreement, among them the mayor and commonality of the city of London, the Dean and Chapter of St Paul's and the Bishop of Winchester. These elaborate rituals continued until the dissolution of the Abbey as a Benedictine monastery in 1540.

The Chapel's nave

THE CHAPEL'S BEAUTIFUL ALTAR as it exists today is similar to the original altar, designed by Torrigiano, which was partly destroyed in 1548 and was finally demolished in the 17th century by the Puritans. The contract for Torrigiano's altar was signed in 1516, by which time Henry VII's chantry and tomb were in position, but he did not begin work on it until 1519. The altar was completed in 1526 and was, like the tomb, part of the vanguard of Renaissance works in 16th-century England. Beneath the altar was an image of the dead Christ in painted terracotta, though there is no surviving picture of it. Though this might seem curious for a Lady altar, the reredos featured a gilt bronze dorsal relief of the Resurrection. But experts point out that this did link in with other features of this altar, including the terracotta dead Christ and the two angels on the canopy holding symbols of the passion, and with the chantry altar, with its piece of the Holy Cross encased in gold.

The present altar, designed by Sir Walter Tapper, was completed in 1935 and incorporates two of the small pillars which supported the original altar table and which survived the Puritan demolition. The altar was the gift of members of the Order of the Bath. The frieze round the canopy incorporates the badge and star of the Order.

Above the altar, instead of the Resurrection, there is a picture of the Madonna and Child by Bartolomeo Vivarini (1432–1499) which was presented by Viscount Lee of Fareham, a Knight of the Bath, in the 1930s.

St Thomas of Canterbury, one of 95 medieval statues in the Chapel.

OPPOSITE: The altar, based on Torrigiano's original design, was installed in 1935.
TOP LEFT: Fifteenth-century Madonna and Child by Bartolomeo Vivarini, given to the Abbey by Viscount Lee of Fareham.

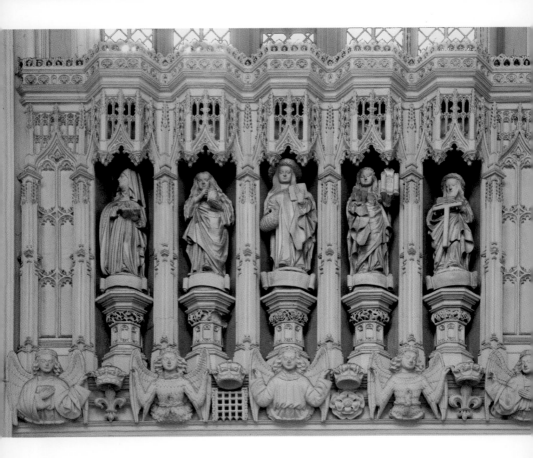

One of the unique features of the Chapel is the wonderful collection of medieval statuary set in niches below the windows which miraculously survived the Puritan desecrations, probably because they were out of reach. Of the original 107 statues, 95 remain. It is the largest and by far the most important surviving collection of sculptured images from Tudor England. They have characteristically strong facial expressions and a variety of intricate headgear. The work is thought to have been done by a workshop of between six to 12 sculptors.

The carvings represent religious figures – the company of Heaven, who would speed the King's soul through purgatory. At the upper level at the east end is Christ flanked by Gabriel and the Blessed Virgin Mary, next come the apostles, then in the nave are the saints, while the western niches contain prophets.

The statues were the ones Henry VII himself had wanted and were probably in place during his lifetime. Among the statues is one of the

Sixteenth-century stalls with the banners of knights of the Most Honourable Order of the Bath above.

OPPOSITE: The medieval statues are a unique survival. The last one on the right is St Wilgeforte with her beard.

female saint, St Wilgeforte or Uncumber, a virgin with a beard, to whom women could pray to rid themselves of their unwanted husbands. Another statue, that of St Sebastian, is flanked by his executioners with crossbows. Two statues show St Matthew wearing spectacles. St Winifred holds a pen and a book and has a female head on a block at her feet. St Agatha is shown in a turban with her right breast exposed, St Roche exposes a boil on his thigh and St Dunstan is holding the devil's nose with a pair of red-hot tongs. At a lower level in the side chapels and aisles are larger sculptures.

On each side of the nave are ornate wooden stalls. Those in the three western bays were in place by the time of the King's death in 1509. Together with those in St George's Chapel, Windsor they are the finest in England. The most striking and unique feature of the stalls is that the rear ones are situated so high – three feet six inches (more than a metre) above the floor. The obvious explanation is that they were designed so that those sitting in

them could see over the top of the chantry, which was originally planned for the centre part of the Chapel. It has also been suggested that the large box-like spaces beneath the stalls acted as sound boxes or 'acoustic chambers', amplifying the sound of the voices of the singers in the stalls.

These stalls were mostly used by the professional choir who sang the elaborate polyphonic daily Lady Mass. Originally the lower stalls (substalls) in the middle bay were omitted, probably to leave enough space around Henry VII's tomb. The fourth (eastern) bay on each side originally contained a stone screen which blocked off access to the Chapel's aisles, but this was replaced in 1725 by a further set of stalls to increase the seating capacity when the Most Honourable Order of the Bath was founded in 1725 (see page 45). To make the canopies over the new stalls, instead of carving them from scratch, the carpenters saved time and money by simply cutting off the backs of the canopies from some of the existing stalls and turning them round. The mutilated backs can be seen from the aisles.

The seats are hinged and, when raised, display a small perching ledge or shelf underneath – a misericord – against which the singers could rest when they had to stand for long periods. They are intricately carved with a range of mostly non-religious motifs including monsters, wildmen, animals and one of a mermaid with her mirror.

The tiny chapel at the extreme east end was dedicated in 1947 in memory of the men of the Royal Air Force who died in the Battle of Britain. This was fought over the south of England from July to October 1940, and proved to be a turning point in the Second World War. Had the battle been lost, and Britain invaded, the consequences for the free world would have been catastrophic. The window, designed by Hugh Easton, depicts the badges of the fighter squadrons which took part in the battle. Four RAF pilots are shown kneeling or standing before visions which symbolise the Redemption. The names of six RAF war leaders are painted

The RAF Chapel, dedicated in 1947, features the Battle of Britain window depicting aircrew. Many gave their lives in defeating the German Luftwaffe, thus saving Britain from invasion.

OPPOSITE: Beneath the seats in the stalls are richly carved misericords featuring a variety of animals and scenes.

below the window. In a Roll of Honour in the Chapel are the names of 1,497 pilots and air crew killed or mortally wounded in the battle. They include men from Great Britain, Australia, New Zealand, Canada, South Africa, Belgium, Czechoslovakia, Poland and one from the United States of America.

Not all those who were buried in Henry VII's Chapel remained there. Oliver Cromwell (died 1658), who ruled over the brief Commonwealth period after Charles I was executed, was given a sumptuous funeral and was buried in a vault at the east end of the Chapel – the effigy on his bier wearing royal robes and a crown. Some of his fellow regicides were also honoured with an Abbey burial, including Henry Ireton (died 1651) and John Bradshaw (died 1659). But in 1661, with the monarchy restored, these three men were exhumed on 26 January in the presence of the Speaker of the House of Commons and his retinue. They were 'taken up, drawn on a hurdle to Tyburn, there to be hanged up in their coffins for some time, after that buried under the gallows'. Their heads were hoisted on poles above Westminster Hall where they remained for at least 20 years. Later in 1661, 23 other leading supporters of the Commonwealth were dug up from the Chapel and cast into St Margaret's Churchyard. Cromwell's erstwhile burial place is now marked with a plaque in the floor just east of Henry VII's chantry.

Oliver Cromwell lay buried in the Abbey until the monarchy was restored when, together with the other regicides, he was exhumed, hanged at Tyburn, decapitated and his body buried beneath the gibbet.

THE BURIAL PLACE OF
OLIVER CROMWELL
1658 · 1661

The Hanoverian burial vault

THE LARGEST BURIAL VAULT IN THE CHAPEL lies under the nave. When George II's wife, Queen Caroline of Ansbach, died on 20 November 1737 the King decided that this new vault should be constructed without delay. Following the decision, the plans for the vault were prepared overnight and, astonishingly, just three weeks later the vault, which occupies virtually the whole of the space beneath the nave floor, had been completed. According to those who have been into the vault it resembles the arcade through the Horseguards in Whitehall. At the east end is a great black and yellow marble sarcophagus two metres by just under one-and-a-half metres (seven feet long and four feet four inches) wide, on which lie specially carved marble crowns, palm branches and sceptres. Caroline was laid to rest in the sarcophagus and was joined 23 years later, in 1760, by her husband. They wanted nothing to separate them after death so the adjacent wooden sides of their coffins were removed and set against the side of the vault where they still rest. It was a symbolic gesture only as the coffins themselves were made of lead which is still intact. In the bays on either side of the vault are other members of George II's family, their names engraved on the Chapel floor directly over where they lie. The coffins were lowered through the floor at the east end of the vault where there was a removable slab.

Funerals in the Abbey were often not without incident and several of those which took place in Henry VII's Chapel gave rise to a certain amount of chaos. After Queen Caroline's funeral, for example, the Dean and Chapter complained to the Earl Marshal that they had been insulted by his secretary at the ceremony. The Earl Marshal promptly sacked him, but reinstated him later when honour was satisfied after he had attended a Chapter meeting and apologised.

After the funeral of the Prince of Wales in the Chapel on 13 April 1751 the Lord Chamberlain, in spite of an earlier agreement, seized the pall and with the help of guards carried it away. The Dean and Chapter then drew up a long document claiming their absolute rights in the Chapel. A few years later, however, there was more trouble.

In 1758, before the funeral of Princess Caroline, one of George II's unmarried daughters, the Lord Chamberlain wrote to the Dean instructing him to deliver the keys of Henry VII's Chapel to the Board of Works so that they might open and close the royal vault in which the Princess was to be interred. The Dean, Zachary Pearce, was furious. He immediately returned the letter explaining that since he was guardian of the royal sepulchres the proper procedure was for the Lord Chamberlain to ask him to order the sepulchre to be opened. The dispute led to a meeting on 4 January in the Deanery attended by the Lord Chamberlain and the Surveyor of the Fabric at which the Lord Chamberlain backed down. A formal letter followed asking the Dean to order the vault to be opened.

Horace Walpole described the chaos of George II's funeral in 1760 in a letter to a friend:

The Royal Standard hangs over the Sovereign's stall at the west end of the Chapel..

'When we came to the Chapel of Henry VII, all solemnity and decorum ceased; no order was observed, people sat or stood where they could or would. The yeoman of the guard were crying out for help, oppressed by the immense weight of the coffin; the bishop read sadly and blundered in the prayers, the fine chapter "Man that is born of a woman" was chanted not read, and the anthem besides being immeasurably tedious, was more fit for a nuptial than a funeral.

'The real serious part was the figure of the Duke of Cumberland … attending the funeral of a father could not be pleasant. His leg extremely bad, yet forced to stand upon it for nearly two hours; his face bloated and distorted with his late paralytic stroke … and placed over the mouth of the vault, into which, in all probability, he must himself so soon descend; think how unpleasant a situation! He bore it all with a firm and unaffected countenance. The grave scene was fully contrasted by the burlesque Duke of Newcastle. He fell into a fit of crying the moment he came into the chapel and flung himself back in a stall, the archbishop hovering over him with a smelling bottle; but in two minutes his curiosity got the better of his hyprocrisy, and he ran about the chapel with his glass to spy who was or was not there, spying with one hand and mopping his eyes with the other. Then returned the fear of catching cold; and the Duke of Cumberland, who was sinking with the heat, felt himself weighed down, and turning round, found it was the Duke of Newcastle standing upon his train, to avoid the chill of the marble. It was very theatric to look down into the vault, where the coffin lay attended by mourners with lights.'

Funerals had their lighter side too. In the vault's south-western bay is the huge coffin containing the remains of William Augustus, Duke of Cumberland (notorious as the 'Butcher of Culloden') the third son of

A model of the Hanoverian burial vault beneath the nave. King George II and Queen Caroline lie in the large sarcophagus on the left.

George II, who died in 1765. Before his funeral, the Dean, Zachary Pearce, received a message: 'Two ladies present their respectful compliments to the Dean of Westminster and would take it as a single favour if his Lordship would break through the usual forms observed on these solemn occasions, and permit them to walk and sing in the procession. They were once too intimately connected with his late Royal Highness. They have remarkably fine voices; are at present sincere Penitents and earnestly wish to offer this last Tribute of Tenderness and Respect to his Memory.' The request was refused.

An unfortunate case of premature entombment

In 1786 during preparations for the funeral of George II's daughter, Princess Amelia, the central stones in the nave floor were removed and a false floor inserted which could be mechanically lowered to sink the coffin in the vault at the appropriate moment during the service. The day before the service, an antiquarian, a Mr Tuffin, bribed one of the workmen to allow him to enter the vault to transcribe some of the inscriptions on the coffins. His stay in the vault was not without incident. Unknown to anyone, a soldier had secreted himself close by and, while Tuffin was quietly making his notes by the light of a wax taper, the soldier began to wrench the silver handle from a neighbouring coffin. Tuffin tackled the soldier, who quickly escaped. Tuffin returned to his researches when, to his horror, he heard the trap door above him being shut, followed shortly by the sound of the great bronze doors to the Chapel being bolted. No-one heard his cries for help. Soon his wax taper burnt out and he found himself entombed in complete darkness with only the coffins of the long dead for company. Thus he remained until the next morning when the vault was once again opened to prepare for the funeral. The reaction of the workmen, who watched an apparently resurrected corpse climbing out, can only be imagined.

Queen Elizabeth's magnificent
tomb in which lies also the body
of her half sister Mary Tudor.
A floor plaque commemorates
those divided at the Reformation
'who laid down their lives for
Christ and conscience sake'.

MEMORIÆ ÆTERNÆ
ELIZABETHÆ ANGLIÆ FRANCIÆ ET HIBERNIÆ
REGINÆ R HENRICI VIII FILIÆ R HEN VII NEPTI R
ED III PRONEPTI INTIMÆ PARENTI RELIGIONIS
ET BONARVM ARTIVM ALTRICI PLVRIMARVM
LINGVARVM PERITIA PRÆCLARIS TVM ANIMI
TVM CORPORIS DOTIBVS REGIISQ VIRTVTIBVS
SVPRA SEXVM PRINCIPI
INCOMPARABILI
IACOBVS MAGNÆ BRITANNIÆ FRANCIÆ ET
HIBERNIÆ REX VIRTVTVM ET REGNORVM
HÆRES BENE MERENTI PIE
POSVIT

Two Queens and 'Innocents Corner'

THE CHAPEL'S AISLES ARE ENTERED through small doorways north and south of the main bronze gates. In the north aisle the most important tomb is that of Queen Elizabeth I. She was crowned in the Abbey in 1559 and reigned for more than 40 years (died 1603). She re-founded the present Abbey in 1560 as the Collegiate Church of St Peter in Westminster.

Her monument, designed by Maximilian Colt and painted by Jan de Critz, was commissioned by James I at the same time as he commissioned a similar yet grander monument to his mother, Mary, Queen of Scots, in the south aisle. Elizabeth's monument was finished in 1606, and created considerable interest at the time. The gilded collar and pendant were added to the effigy in 1975 to replace items stolen before 1723. The gilded crown was added more recently. The original railings round the tomb were removed in 1822 but new ones were placed here in 1983.

The crown, collar and pendant on Elizabeth I's effigy on her tomb were added in recent times to replace the long lost originals.

In the vault beneath, Queen Elizabeth's coffin lies directly on top of that of her half-sister, Mary (died 1558) who had restored England to the Roman Catholic faith after the death of Edward VI, and had terrorised Protestants, burning 300 of them at the stake as heretics. A Latin inscription encompasses both sisters: 'Partners in throne and grave, here we sleep, Elizabeth and Mary, sisters in hope of the resurrection.' In 1977 a floor stone was unveiled, commemorating those who were divided at the Reformation 'who laid down their lives for Christ and conscience sake'.

At the far east end of the north aisle is a group of monuments which has led this area to be called 'Innocents' Corner'. Here lie the remains of children, two of whom died of natural causes, two of whom were murdered. All have eloquent memorials which speak of bitter grief.

In a casket set into the wall are said to be the bones of the 'Princes in the Tower' – the boy king, Edward V, and his brother, Richard, Duke of York – who were murdered in the Tower of London sometime in 1483. They were the sons of King Edward IV and his beloved wife Elizabeth Woodville.

Edward IV had died in 1483, aged just 41, and was succeeded by his 12-year-old son, Edward. Too young to rule, he was in the official care of his uncle, Richard of Gloucester, a ruthless and ambitious man who had his eye on the throne himself. Richard brought the young King to London and lodged him the Tower. Meanwhile, Edward IV's widow, fearing for her life, claimed sanctuary in Westminster Abbey together with her five daughters and her other son, the nine-year-old Richard, Duke of York. Richard of Gloucester now schemed to remove him as well and, with the Archbishop of Canterbury as his emissary, persuaded Elizabeth Woodville to allow the young Duke to join his brother in the Tower to be a play-mate for him. Elizabeth tearfully said good-bye to him. '"Farewell mine own sweet son, God send you a good keeping: let me kiss you yet once, ere you go, for God knoweth when wee shall kiss together againe." And

The inscription on the tomb translates as 'Partners in throne and grave, here we sleep, Elizabeth and Mary, sisters in hope of the Resurrection.'

REGNO CONSORES
&VRNA HIC OBDOR
MIMVS ELIZABETHA

ET MARIA SORORES
IN SPE RESVRREC=
TIONIS

The supposed remains of the
murdered Princes in the Tower
(top left), Princess Maria (above)
and Princess Sophia,
the daughters of James I,
lie in 'Innocent's Corner'.

therewithall she kissed him, and blessed him, turned her back and wept, and went on her way, leaving the child weeping as fast.' The two boys were last seen playing together in the Tower in the summer of 1483 and, it is surmised, were probably killed some time in August that year.

Nearly 200 years later, in 1674, a collection of bones in an elm chest was dug up from beneath a staircase in the Tower and assumed to be the bones of the Princes. On the orders of Charles II, they were placed in a casket which was set into the wall in Henry VII Chapel.

In July 1933 the casket was opened and the contents examined by experts to try to verify whether these were indeed the Princes' remains. There were a number of bones, including the skulls, jawbones and thigh bones of two children of about the same age as the two princes and, because of certain similarities in the skulls, the experts concluded that they were probably related. Also in the casket were a number of animal bones and some rusty nails. Curiously, the investigation made no attempt to determine whether the bones were male or female. If a similar investigation were carried out today a great deal more information could be gleaned, including confirmation of the sex of the bones and also DNA evidence showing whether the two individuals were related. Though the experts concluded that the claim that the bones were those of the Princes in the Tower remained 'not proven', it seems likely.

Also at the east end of the aisle are two monuments, by Maximilian Colt, to infant daughters of James I. The first, Princess Sophia, died in 1606 aged three days and is represented, as her father had wished, lying in an alabaster cradle. A Latin inscription translates as 'A royal rosebud, untimely plucked by death; torn from her parents to bloom afresh in the rose garden of Christ'. Close by is the tomb of her sister, Princess Mary, who died in 1607 aged two years. She reclines on her elbow on a small altar tomb. Her father described her as 'a most beautiful infant'. At her death she apparently kept repeating, 'I go, I go, away I go.'

The Stuarts and Mary, Queen of Scots

THE FIRST PERSON TO BE BURIED in the south aisle of the Chapel was Henry VII's mother, Lady Margaret Beaufort (died 1509). A wealthy lady, she married four times, founded two Cambridge Colleges, Christ's and St John's, the Chairs of Divinity at both Oxford and Cambridge and she established various charities. She also helped pay for the Chapel. At her funeral, her friend and confessor Bishop Fisher, said, 'Everyone that knew her loved her, and everything that she said or did became her'. She died in what is now the Abbey's Deanery. The work on the tomb was carried out by Torrigiano and her portrait effigy in old age is said to be Torrigiano's masterpiece. The metal railings round the tomb had been sold in 1823 but were returned to the Abbey in 1915 after being bought by the National Art Collections Fund. They had originally been painted and decorated with coats of arms and fleurs de lis and other ornaments.

Following Lady Margaret Beaufort's death, there were no further burials in this aisle for nearly 70 years until the burial of Margaret, Countess of Lennox (died 1578), the grand-daughter of Henry VII. Her sons and daughters are depicted as weepers or mourners either side of the monument. Like many others in the Abbey, this monument has suffered damage over the years, not least at the hands of souvenir hunters. In the 1950s it was repaired and re-coloured but since then further damage has been done. The hands went missing from two of the figures and the unicorn heraldic devices lost their horns. On the south side of the tomb is one weeper, Lord Darnley, the husband of Mary, Queen of Scots, with a crown over his head. His crown, replaced in 1957, later lost its cross.

At the far east end of the south aisle beneath the floor is the Stuart Vault containing the bodies of Charles II (died 1685), Mary II (died 1694), William III (died 1702), Prince George of Denmark (died 1708), who was Queen Anne's husband, and Queen Anne herself (died 1714). She was a particularly large lady and the other coffins had to be shifted along a little to allow room for her own much larger one. This vault was entered by Dean Stanley in 1869 in his search for the coffin of James I (which was eventually found in Henry VII's burial vault). It was last entered in 1976

OPPOSITE: Henry VII's mother, the wealthy Lady Margaret Beaufort, died in the Abbot's lodgings (now the Deanery) in 1509. Her effigy and tomb are by Pietro Torrigiano.

The tomb of Mary, Queen of
Scots, was commissioned by
her son James I, who brought
her body to the Abbey from
Peterborough Cathedral in 1612.

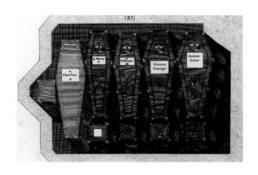

to investigate a suspected gas leak. The wax deposits left by Dean Stanley's candles 100 years before were still visible on the coffins. Charles II's coffin was seen to have collapsed and his remains were visible, as were some of the clothes in which he was buried, including his buckled shoes. The Dean at the time, Dr Edward Carpenter, said later that he had favoured tidying things up and repairing the coffin but one of the conditions laid down by Her Majesty The Queen, when permission was sought and given to open the vault, was that nothing should be touched – and so it was left as it was found. West of this tomb is that of Mary, Queen of Scots (1542–1587). Mary was the daughter of James V of Scotland and Mary of Guise. She was educated at the French Court but left France for Scotland on the death of her first husband, Francis II. In 1568 she was captured by the English and after 19 years' imprisonment was executed at Fotheringhay Castle in 1587 under a warrant signed by Queen Elizabeth I, to whom she was considered a threat. She was buried first at Peterborough Cathedral but in 1612 her son James I brought her remains to Westminster and placed them beneath a grand monument he commissioned from Cornelius Cure. Her effigy is of white marble and at her feet sits the Scottish lion crowned. The vault beneath contains, among others, four children of Charles I, two of James I and some fourteen children of Queen Anne, none of whom survived infancy.

Above the altar at the east end of the aisle is a tapestry of wool, silk and silver gilt. It represents the Descent from the Cross and is thought to be Flemish dating from the early part of the 16th century. It was given to the Abbey in 1929 by the Duke of Westminster in memory of his mother, the Countess Grosvenor.

Eighteenth-century plan of burials in the Stuart vault. When the vault was entered in 1976 Charles II's coffin was seen to have collapsed, revealing his remains.

The 'decaying' Chapel restored

JUST AS THE INSIDE OF THE CHAPEL is a feast for the eye, so the exterior is equally impressive, with a remarkable series of carvings of Tudor emblems and animals. Over the centuries the Caen and Reigate stone deteriorated in the acidic London air and major renovation became necessary. At one stage some of the statues on the outside had to be removed 'in case they fell on the heads of those attending Parliament'. In the later seventeenth and early eighteenth centuries Christopher Wren, the Abbey's first Surveyor of the Fabric, and Nicholas Hawksmoor, his assistant had, at different times, provided estimates of what it would cost to restore the Chapel, but nothing was done.

Towards the end of the eighteenth century the Chapel suffered further decay until, in 1793, James Wyatt, the Surveyor, at last began some repairs. But a fire in the lantern on 9 July 1803 led to most of the money earmarked for the Chapel being used to repair the fire damage, and the deterioration continued.

At last, in 1806, Parliament stepped in and the new Prime Minister, Lord Grenville, and his so-called 'Ministry of All the Talents' began providing Government money for the Chapel's restoration. It was to take 15 years, but still things did not go smoothly. A shipment of 150 tons of stone, being brought to the Abbey for the Chapel, sank in a storm. To make matters worse, neither the ship nor the cargo was insured. Eventually more stone was procured and the work completed in 1822.

By 1852, the stone was once more decaying. The details of the carving were becoming so obscured that the Abbey's Surveyor, George Gilbert Scott, forecast that within a century it would become a 'mere mouldering mass'. It was not until 1929 that the first systematic campaign of repair for a century was begun by the then Surveyor of the Fabric, Walter Tapper. But there was more trouble in store. On 29 August 1932 one of the cusps inside the Chapel, weighing some 10 pounds, crashed down near the altar. The Chapel was closed and remained so for two years while the structure was strengthened.

As war broke out, many of the moveable valuables were evacuated – a wise precaution, as in September 1940 a bomb fell close by, blowing out nearly all the Chapel's glass and sending two pendants crashing from the vault. In the 1990s a major restoration was carried out when some 800 new carvings replaced those on the outside which had been eaten away. The Chapel is now in as good a state as it has ever been.

One of some 800 new carvings on the outside of the Chapel which replaced those damaged by London's acidic atmosphere.

OPPOSITE: Mary Queen of Scots was executed on Elizabeth I's orders in 1587. Her white marble effigy shows her wearing a close fitting coif and laced ruff.

The Most Honourable Order of the Bath

THE BRIGHTLY COLOURED BANNERS hanging on each side of the Chapel belong to the Knights Grand Cross of the Most Honourable Order of the Bath. The curious name harks back to before the reign of Henry IV (crowned 1399) when, before they received the accolade, new knights had to undergo a ritual bath, symbolic of spiritual washing or baptism, followed by a night of prayer and meditation.

The Order was officially established by George I in 1725. The then Prime Minister, Robert Walpole, was keen to see the Order of Knighthood established so that he could ensure support in the House of Commons and House of Lords from those he so honoured. Today the honour is mainly awarded to serving officers of the armed forces and to a limited number of senior civil servants. The Order of Knighthood is headed by the Great Master, currently the Prince of Wales. The Dean of Westminster is Dean of the Order and wears the badge of office whenever he wears his robes, and Henry VII Chapel is the designated Chapel of the Order. The link with the medieval knights is purely symbolic and there is no real connection. Though the 1725 statutes set out precisely the details of the

The coats of arms on the knights' banners reflect their career and interests.

LEFT: Newly installed knights in the Abbey's Jerusalem Chamber with The Queen and Charles, Prince of Wales, the Order's Great Master.
OPPOSITE: Canaletto's painting of the procession of Knights of the Most Honourable Order of the Bath leaving the Abbey after an installation service in 1749.

45

The knights' crests above
their stalls and their banners
are returned to their families
after their deaths, while their
enamel stall plates remain
as a permanent memorial.

bath to be taken and the night-long vigil, the statutes also allowed these obligations to be dispensed with and, in practice, none of the knights had to undergo such rigours.

Until 1725 there were only 24 stalls (12 each side) in the western three bays of the Chapel. But in 1725 the stone screens in the next bay along on each side were removed and an extra five stalls were added on each side, making a total of 34, to accomodate 34 knights.

Installations took place until 1812 but were then suspended because in 1815 the Order was enlarged to three classes and so many new knights were created that it was no longer praticable to install them. So, just as the need for a bath and a vigil had been dispensed with earlier, now the installation ceremonies themselves were also dispensed with. The old banners were left in place and, over the next century, fell into tatters. By 1913 they were a very sorry sight.

Then, in 1913, the colourfull installation ceremonies were restarted and now take place once every four years, with the most senior knights taking over the stalls left vacant by the death of their previous occupants. Originally an exclusively military order, in 1815 the Civil Division was created – mainly for senior civil servants. Today the stalls are allocated in the proportion 26 military to 8 civil. Newly created knights can wait a long time for their stall. Field Marshal Sir Gerald Templer and Lord Mountbatten of Burma were appointed Knights in 1955 but had to wait until 1972 to be installed.

In the 18th century, galleries were built in Henry VII Chapel so that family and friends could witness the ceremony. Today the service takes place in the main Abbey; during which all the existing knights and those to be installed process up to the Chapel for the installation ceremony. As part of the ceremony the knights take the oath, which includes a pledge to honour God above all things, be steadfast in the faith of Christ, honour The Queen and defend maidens, widows and orphans. The knights are then seated in their stalls by the Great Master. After this, first the Sovereign, then the Great Master, make an offering of gold and silver at the altar. The Great Master draws his sword and presents it to the Dean, who lays it on the altar and then returns it exhorting him, and the other knights, to use their swords 'to the Glory of God, the Defence of the Gospel, the maintenance of your Sovereign's Right and Honour, and of all Equity and Justice to the utmost of your power'.

Above each stall is the knight's banner, crest and mantle (symbolic of the cloth that would have protected the knight in his armour from sun or rain), while his enamelled stall plate, bearing his coat of arms, is fastened to the back of the stall. When a knight dies, his banner, crest and mantle are taken down and given to his family; his stall plate remains as a permanent memorial.

Her Majesty The Queen leaves the Abbey after an installation service.

Acknowledgements

I am grateful to the following for their help: The Dean and Chapter of Westminster, Richard Mortimer, Tim Tatton-Brown, Christine Reynolds, Sal Shuel, Simon Shuel, Gill Gibbins, Douglas East, Malcolm Crowthers, Jacques Heyman (for permission to use his illustration at the top of page 12), and Andrew Dunsmore.

I also acknowledge with gratitude the following sources of information:

Westminster Abbey: The Lady Chapel of Henry VII, edited by Tim Tatton-Brown and Richard Mortimer;

The Westminster Abbey Official Guide;

The Sculptural Decoration of the Henry VII Chapel Westminster Abbey by Helen J Dowe;

articles in *The Westminster Abbey Chorister* magazine.

Picture acknowledgements:

Angelo Hornak: 19, 24, 37 (effigies).

Picture Partnership: 45 (group), 47.

Malcolm Crowthers: 3, 5, 6, 7, 9, 11, 14, 17, 30, 32, 33, 43, 46, back cover.

All other images © Dean and Chapter of Westminster.

First published 2007
New edition 2013
New edition 2017

ISBN 0–9552470–2–0
987–0–9552470–2–6

Design: Bridget Heal
Publisher: Tudsbury Press, 31 Elm Bank Gardens, Barnes, London SW13 0NU
Printer: G H Smith & Son, Market Place, Easingwold, York YO61 3AB

BACK COVER: Gilt bronze putti guard each corner of Henry VII's remarkable Renaissance tomb.